WHO, WHAT, WHY?

WHY DID

Slavery End?

DANIKA COOLEY

CF4•K

10 9 8 7 6 5 4 3 2 1
Copyright © Danika Cooley 2023
Paperback ISBN: 978-1-5271-1011-3
ebook ISBN: 978-1-5271-1079-3

Published by
Christian Focus Publications,
Geanies House, Fearn, Tain, Ross-shire,
IV20 1TW, Scotland, U.K.
www.christianfocus.com
email: info@christianfocus.com

Printed and bound by Bell and Bain, Glasgow

Cover design by Catriona Mackenzie
Illustrations by Martyn Smith

TABLE OF CONTENTS

Dedication

To the Reader (That's you!)
May you love your neighbor faithfully.

THE AUTHOR

Danika Cooley and her husband, Ed, are committed to leading their children to life for the glory of God. Danika has a passion for equipping parents to teach the Bible and Christian history to their kids. She is the author of *Help Your Kids Learn and Love the Bible, When Lightning Struck!: The Story of Martin Luther, Wonderfully Made: God's Story of Life from Conception to Birth,* and the *Who, What, Why?* Series about the history of our faith. Danika's three year Bible survey curriculum, Bible Road Trip™, is used by families around the world. Weekly, she encourages tens of thousands of parents to intentionally raise biblically literate children. Danika is a homeschool mother of four with a bachelor of arts degree from the University of Washington. Find her at ThinkingKidsBlog.org.

THE FREEING
OF GOD'S IMAGE BEARERS

A long time ago, in Israel, a scribe asked Jesus what the most important command of all is. Jesus said: "You shall love the Lord your God with all your heart and with all your soul and with all your mind and with all your strength." The second is this: "You shall love your neighbor as yourself" (Mark 12:29b-31a). Love God and love others. That doesn't sound too hard, does it?

Have you ever ignored a dirty sock on the bathroom floor, stepping around it for days? People do that with sin, too. But sin is much worse than a filthy sock. Sin violates God's laws and separates us from him. Sin hurts other people—it is the opposite of love. We are going to look at an ugly sin that was ignored not just for days, but centuries. However, God's people loved their neighbors—and their neighborly love changed history.

Even though God created us to love each other, some wicked people kidnapped other people and forced them to work. We call that slavery. Slavery hurts human beings. For a while, Christians ignored that slavery is wrong and pretended that people with skin that was a different color than theirs were not their neighbors. Then, God's people remembered they must fight for justice and truth—they must love their neighbors. All people are image bearers—created in the image of God.

Slavery has been around for a very long time. Maybe you remember the story of Joseph, the son of Jacob? Joseph's brothers were jealous of the dreams God gave him, so they attacked Joseph and sold him to Ishmaelite merchants, who then sold Joseph as a slave in Egypt. Eventually, all of Jacob's descendants, the

Israelites, were slaves in Egypt until God freed them in the Exodus.

After that, the history of slavery is a bit of a mess, even for careful history detectives like you. Slavery was everywhere. African tribes enslaved each other. North Africans enslaved the British and Irish. Ancient Greeks and Romans took slaves from parts of Africa, Asia, and the Middle East. Muslims from the Middle East took slaves from Africa, Europe, and Asia. Europeans enslaved each other. Do you know the story of Patrick? He was a slave stolen from England and taken to Ireland.

Then, eleven years before the Gutenberg Bible was printed on the very first printing press, Prince Henry the Navigator of Portugal—who had been sailing around growing sugar cane on islands for some twenty-four years—kidnapped two hundred and forty Africans. Prince Henry kept kidnapping Africans, about eight hundred each year. By the time Martin Luther nailed The Ninety-Five Theses to the door of the Wittenberg Castle Church in Germany, telling people that we are saved in Christ alone by grace alone through faith alone, a Roman Catholic bishop in Spain told people to grab free workers in Africa.

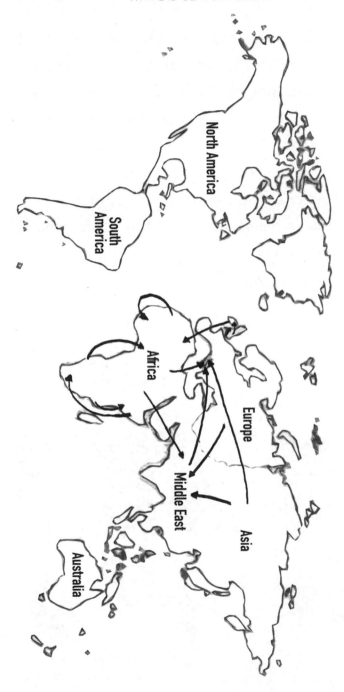

When Europeans sailed to the New World—the Americas and the islands of the Atlantic—some people were looking for the freedom to worship Jesus, but others were looking for land, gold, and crops. Of course, anyone who is going to farm a tropical paradise needs workers. At first, no one cared what color skin their slaves had. Black, white, or native men could be explorers or farmers, enslaved or free. Unfortunately, kidnapped laborers died—often. The plantation owners needed to kidnap a lot more free workers.

If you spend time looking at a map, you'll see that Africa is huge, with fifty-four countries on the continent. There were millions of Africans to kidnap. So, that's what the kidnappers did.

As the Reformer John Knox was telling the people of Scotland about the good news of Jesus Christ, sailors enslaved ten thousand people a year to work in the New World. They sailed from port to port, packing their ships with five hundred Africans, like sardines in a can. By the time Christians began to organize to protest enslavement, over thirty thousand Africans per year were being shipped into lives of forced servitude. Just twelve years later, the number had increased to fifty thousand each year. By the time of the American Revolution, more than seventy-five thousand people were kidnapped each year from Africa and forced to work in fields, stores, and homes in the Americas.

The Americas were colonized—that means settled— by Western European countries like Britain, Spain, Portugal, and France. By 1772—just four years before the American Revolution, if you were free, standing in a room with twenty-three people, you could be the only free person in the entire room. It was a mess.

People were sinning all over the place. They were kidnapping others and buying people as if they were cows or sheep. Families were separated from each other, people were abused, and slave owners refused to let slaves read God's Word or pray.

The big fight to end slavery lasted two hundred years—from AD 1688 until 1888. This is the story of how—and why—global slavery ended. It's the story of Christians who loved their neighbors with their whole lives and brave, enslaved men, women, and children who fought for the freedom of their neighbors.

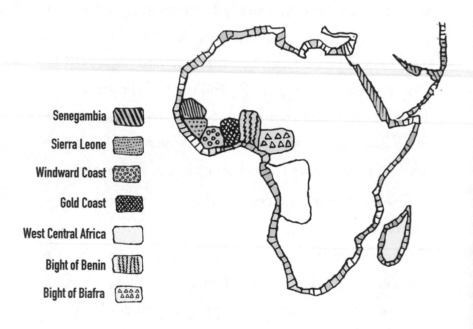

Senegambia
Sierra Leone
Windward Coast
Gold Coast
West Central Africa
Bight of Benin
Bight of Biafra

Places from which enslaved people departed Africa by ship.

WORKING FOR FREEDOM

We become Christians when we repent—turn away from our sins—and believe in Jesus. Christians are commanded to love biblical justice, to protect others, and to speak for people in need. Freeing the enslaved was a big job. People who loved their neighbors enough to spend their lives working to abolish—or end—slavery are called abolitionists.

For two hundred years, Christians used Scripture to write arguments against kidnapping and abuse. They pressured governments to abolish the slave trade— kidnapping and shipping Africans overseas. Escaped slaves told the story of how God protected and freed them. Lawyers fought to free—or emancipate— enslaved people after the end of the slave trade. In some countries, many people died in battle to end slavery.

GOD HOLDS
BACK SIN

Has your mom ever told you, "Don't hit your brother!" or, "Speak kindly to your sister!"? You were probably already being unkind, right? When your mom or dad tells you not to do something specific, they are holding back your sin. There's a big word for that—constraining.

The first sin—the one that makes you think it is okay to hit or yell—is your anger. Jesus said that to insult

your brother or call him names in anger is a sin equal to murder in your heart (Matthew 5:21-26). Whoa! God condemns that sin—it is not allowed.

So why does your mom say, "Don't hit!" instead of "Don't be angry!"? Instead of condemning— disapproving of—the sin in your heart, your mom is addressing your sinful behavior. She is holding back your anger—or constraining sin. God does the same thing in his law.

Exodus chapters 20-24 make up what theologians— people who study God and his Word—call the Book of the Covenant. It is God's law to his nation, Israel. First, God gave the Israelites ten rules to live by called the Ten Commandments.

The eighth Commandment says, "You shall not steal." Maybe you think of stealing as taking candy that doesn't belong to you. You've probably never thought about taking a whole person before. God, though, tells us not to steal people. In Exodus 21:16, God gives a very direct order, condemning sin: "Whoever steals a man and sells him,

and anyone found in possession of him, shall be put to death." God makes kidnapping and the slave trade illegal, punishable by death.

God also constrains sin by putting rules on slavery. The seventh year, the enslaved person goes free—without paying a ransom. God says, too, that any slave who is hurt by a master must be set free, protecting slaves from abuse.

God condemns slavery again in the New Testament, his instructions to today's Church. In his first letter to Timothy, Paul tells Timothy to instruct the Ephesian Christians that we must love others. Then, Paul says that God gave us the law to constrain—hold back—people from sin. The law is for sinners so that they will know they are sinning, and they need Jesus. Paul lists

different kinds of people living in disobedience to God. One type of sinner Paul names is an "enslaver."

Now, Paul did not write his letter in English. Instead, he wrote it in Greek so that many people at that time could understand it. The word he used for enslaver was a combination of two Greek words put together to

mean "man-stealer." God's Word is clear. People who steal other people are living against God's law. They are opposed to God—not walking in his will or in the salvation of Jesus.

Sometimes people point out that God himself ordered the enslavement of some people groups in the Old Testament. That is true, but that was a one-time event. The people had badly sinned against God in terrible ways. Their enslavement was a special punishment from God for their horrible treatment of the King of the Universe and his people.

You should know, too, that slavery in the Bible was different than slavery during the time of abolition. People in biblical times could enter slavery when they owed money or as a punishment for stealing. The idea of just war—a moral war—is something theologians have debated for centuries. Sometimes, as with the Canaanites, people were enslaved because they sinned grievously. In the ancient world, bondservants were treated much like a member of the family. They were often educated or specially trained. It could be safer to be a bondservant than to be poor and without family—it was a way to avoid starving. Sometimes people became bondservants willingly.

Over time, the nature of slavery changed. Historians call this new kind of bondage chattel slavery. The word chattel means property. That is exactly how chattel slaves were treated—like property—for their entire lives. Chattel slaves could not own property, testify in court, get help from police, legally marry, or travel without a permit. People held in chattel slavery were often horribly abused. Children were born into slavery and frequently sold away from their parents. Especially in Europe and its territories, people were enslaved according to the color of their skin, which made it easy to see who was enslaved and who was not.

In his Word, God tells us how to live so that we will love God and love others. Then, he gives us even more instruction to constrain—hold back—our sin to keep us from hurting the people we are supposed to love. Many people have tried to confuse God's Word by telling others that God allows and encourages slavery. Really, God is very clear that man-stealing and selling human beings is a grave sin—and a crime. God is also clear that to harm a slave, even by knocking out their tooth, is a sin so big that the person should immediately be freed.

HATING THE SIN

Some of the first abolitionists were Quakers, like Benjamin Lay who smashed his wife's teacups to protest sugar grown with slave labor. Most Quakers hated slavery. They led the abolition movement early on by forming societies and launching petitions.

Quakers are a religious sect that began during the Reformation. After the end of the Reformation, the Quaker movement faced charges of heresy in England. Quakers say that Jesus lives in all people—whether they have repented of sin or not. They allow all members to speak at meetings as if they were speaking for the Lord. These teachings are not what the Bible teaches.

EUROPE AND
THE ISLANDS

Slavery in the West Indies made plantation owners lots of money. Planters would occasionally sail home to Europe, bringing a slave or two with them. People in Europe wanted slavery to be far away, across the ocean. So, Europeans declared their own cities—and then countries—to be "free soil." Abolitionists, though, didn't forget about enslaved people. They believed that Jesus frees us from our sins—and we should all be free from actual chains as well.

PORTUGAL

Roman Catholic Spain and Portugal wanted to use slaves to operate plantations, so they asked Pope Julius II to approve the slave trade—kidnapping and selling people— as a way to bring people to Jesus. Now, if kidnapping people sounds like a weird way to share the good news of Jesus, that's because it is. By the end of the American Revolution, Portugal had freed all slaves inside their country—and banned any free black people from entering. By 1815, after five hundred years of enslaving Africans, Portugal agreed to abolish the slave trade.

THE BRITISH EMPIRE

By 1922, the British Empire ruled one quarter of the earth, including much of the West Indies—now called the Caribbean Islands. The abolitionist movement in Britain was mostly political and legal.

Just before America won freedom from Britain in the Revolutionary War, an enslaved man named James Somerset sued in court for his freedom. The judge said slavery was hateful and "the black" must be freed. Now, maybe the judge meant only the "black" James Somerset, but black people in England believed all blacks would be freed. The Somerset case did not free all British slaves, so Christian British abolitionists worked even harder.

The British Government abolished the slave trade in 1807. Still, slavery continued in the British territories for years afterward. Right after Christmas in Jamaica in 1831, a Baptist deacon organized enslaved Jamaicans to go on strike from work. Instead, they burned so many plantations it looked like the sky was on fire. Planters then killed over five hundred slaves and threw missionaries out of the country. What the plantation owners meant for evil, God used for good when over a million British men and women signed a petition against all British slavery.

Once the English people were convinced that slavery is wrong, they wanted other countries to abandon enslaving others, too, and they used their Navy to patrol the oceans and free prisoners on slave ships. Then, on August 1, 1834, around eight hundred thousand British slaves were freed in twenty-four colonies. Across the world, people everywhere celebrated Emancipation Day as a holiday on the first of August each year.

SPAIN

Pressured by Britain, in 1817 Spain agreed to stop shipping Africans to Cuba, Puerto Rico, and other islands north of the Equator. But, Spain secretly continued their slave trade. Spanish and Portuguese abolitionists fought for the freedom of hundreds of thousands of slaves in Cuba, Puerto Rico, and South America. Slavery in Spanish territories ended unevenly as South American countries won independence from Spain through warfare. Puerto Ricans were freed in 1873. After a ten-year war, Spain ended all Cuban slavery in 1886.

DENMARK AND THE NETHERLANDS

Like the other Western European countries that had access to waterways, Denmark and the Netherlands used their resources to begin kidnapping and selling Africans into forced labor in the West Indies and parts of Africa just after the Reformation ended. Denmark abolished the slave trade by 1792, but it wasn't until 1807 that Denmark freed all slaves. The Netherlands did not free slaves until 1873, the same year one of the largest slave markets in the world—in Zanzibar, Tanzania—was closed.

FRANCE

France benefited from slavery more than any other European country. Slaves brought to the country from colonial areas sued for freedom—and won. But, in 1777, France ruled all black people were created to be slaves.

This logic was also used in Portugal, Spain, and the United States, where the color of one's skin became a justification for slavery.

Abolition in France was forgotten as the country plunged into the French Revolution. In ten years, over twenty thousand French people were killed and Napoleon Bonaparte took charge of the country. Even during the Revolution, France still shipped over two million Africans into slavery every year. In 1791, the people of Haiti—France's most valuable colony—decided they'd had enough of being enslaved.

Haitian slaves burned more than one thousand plantations in a month. Hundreds of slaves and

enslavers were killed. The French legislature offered free blacks citizenship, French troops invaded the island, and ten thousand whites fled. It took years of back-and-forth struggle throughout the French islands to abolish slavery. Haiti finally became its own country in 1804. Forty-four years later, a small band of abolitionists—and many enslaved Africans who revolted—succeeded in convincing France to free all Caribbean slaves.

Though slaves in European territories were freed by the late 1800s, those same countries continued systems of forced labor in other areas of the world. No one dreamed that in the early-to mid-1900s, Europe itself would become the scene of mass slavery.

GOOD NEWS FOR EVERYONE

During the First Great Awakening, which started in 1730, up to fifty thousand people came to salvation in Jesus while George Whitefield, Jonathan Edwards, and others preached. New Divinity preachers—followers of Edwards'—then called people to repent and to love their neighbors with real action.

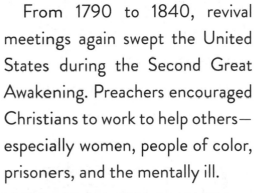

From 1790 to 1840, revival meetings again swept the United States during the Second Great Awakening. Preachers encouraged Christians to work to help others— especially women, people of color, prisoners, and the mentally ill.

Throughout abolition, Christians on both sides of the Atlantic preached and wrote warnings about God's justice. They called all Christians to repent of slavery. After all, every human is created in the image of God, and every person is our neighbor.

31

MADE IN THE
IMAGE OF GOD

Do you know the story of God's Creation of the earth? God tells us this story in the first two chapters of the Bible, in the book of Genesis. Maybe you've memorized the first verse of Genesis: "In the beginning, God created the heavens and the earth." God created all things, and no one created God. God always has been and always will be.

When God was creating the heavens and the earth, he made a beautiful place for us to live, full of everything we would need to survive and be happy, like oxygen, plants, water, and animals. God created each living thing according to its kind. So, zebras and horses are similar, but not at all like alligators or crocodiles. Each living thing has a family of sorts.

Next, God made a man, whom he named Adam, and Adam's wife, Eve. Genesis 1:27 says: "So God created man in his own image, in the image of God he created him; male and female he created them." Humans were their own kind—or family, made as a

representation of God. Theologians love to name big truths. They especially love to name big truths in Latin, an old language no one uses anymore. The term *imago Dei*—which is Latin for image of God—signifies the big truth that every human is created by God in his own image.

God charged humans with caring for the earth and the animals in it. He also told people to work—and showed them the example of taking one day each week to rest. God expects people to love and care for his creation, not to harm or abuse it.

God also gave humans the gift of being male or female, and of marriage and family. God told humans to multiply and fill the earth. We are to love and care especially for the families God gives us. One of the evils of slavery is that the enslaved people are often robbed of God's special gift of marriage and children. This destruction of families and marriages is a terrible sin that should hurt the heart of everyone who loves God and values his perfect design.

In the New Testament, God gives us the special gift of our Church family—other Christians become our brothers and sisters in Christ. Do you remember that Jesus said, "You shall love your neighbor as yourself."? Well, we are to love all people as we love ourselves. In

1 John 3:16, John adds: "By this we know love, that he laid down his life for us, and we ought to lay down our lives for the brothers." Jesus sacrificed everything for Christians, and God wants us to love our Christian brothers and sisters so much we will sacrifice everything for each other.

There's more. We know that we are *imago Dei*—
made in the image of God. In the book of Acts, Luke
tells us the people of Athens did not know who God—
the King of the Universe—is, but they had an altar
to the "unknown god." When Paul saw that altar, he
told the Athenians the Creation story from the first
chapter of Genesis. He said the God who made the
world and everything in it is the Lord of heaven and
earth. Then, Paul explained that God gave breath to
all mankind. In fact, God made every nation from just
one man.

All nations came from Adam.

That means it doesn't matter what color your skin is or what continent or nation your family is from. What matters is that God made you as one of his people, in his own image. All people are *imago Dei*—made in the image of God. All humans are special to our King.

Have you ever tried to count the hairs on your head? It would be an impossible task. But, the Bible says God knows the number of hairs each person has on top of their head. That is how much the King of the Universe cares for each person he made in his own image. Not only that, God paid the sin of each of those he calls his child through the sacrifice of Jesus, who is God the Son and the Son of God. When John tells us to lay down our lives for the brothers, he is talking about sacrificing for other Christians the way Jesus sacrificed for us. Jesus died in the place of every Christian, taking the punishment for their sins. Then, he rose from the dead. Now, John knows you and I can't forgive anyone's sin. But, we can love each other so much we can give our time, energy, or favorite shirt to another Christian in need.

That's what the abolitionists did. They spent their whole lives working to help their enslaved brothers and sisters. Abolitionists suffered for the good of others. They surrendered their lives to God in their love for their neighbors. God does not intend for us to treat each other poorly based on race, ethnicity, or nationality. All people are made in the image of God, and all skin colors show God's creative majesty.

DEAR GOVERNMENT

A petition is a request written to a government and signed by citizens. During the 1833 session of British Parliament, four men lugged in massive stacks of paper filled with anti-slavery signatures from all over Britain. Surprised members of Parliament clapped as they realized enslaved people in the West Indies would finally be freed.

American abolitionists sent petition after petition to Congress. Many congressional members were from the slave-owning South. Congress made a gag rule that said no member of Congress could discuss, vote on, or even read the petitions they received. Americans from northern states saw the gag rule as a challenge. They quickly sent more than six hundred thousand petitions with almost two million signatures to Congress and state governments.

THE FREEING
OF THE AMERICAS

Many of the countries of North, Central, and South America gained their independence from Europe, then fought to retain slavery. Only after struggle, and sometimes war, were the people of the Americas freed.

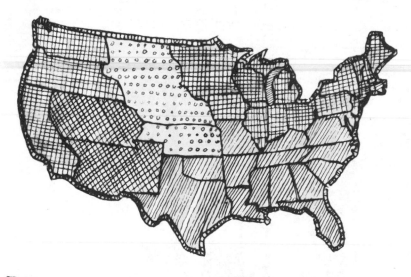

 Free States & Territories 1864

 Open to Slavery by Kansas Nebraska Act 1854

Open to Slavery by Compromise of 1850

 Slave States & Territories

United States of America

CANADA

A little over forty years after the United States won their independence from Britain in 1819, Britain declared that Canada, a British territory, was a safe place for all blacks to live. Because Britain refused to allow Americans to recapture fugitive slaves who escaped into Canada, many runaway slaves established colonies north of the land of their enslavement. Native Americans enslaved in Canada celebrated Emancipation Day with the British island territories on August 1, 1834.

THE UNITED STATES OF AMERICA

Before the Revolutionary War, as Quakers argued for abolition, Protestant ministers preached on the evils of slavery and wrote about God's love for all people. During the war, British troops promised freedom to any enslaved man who fought for the British Army. Slaves also fled, joining maroon communities in swamps and forests—even in Mexico. As many as seventy thousand enslaved people found freedom over the course of the war.

Shortly after the war, northern states banned slavery. Southern states made lots of money from cotton raised on plantations, so they imported more slaves. As America expanded westward, people argued

over allowing slavery
in each new state. In
the North, Christian
abolitionists ran
newspapers and
toured northern
states, writing
and speaking about
ending slavery.

Though the
United States banned the slave trade in 1808, things
were a mess. New slaves couldn't be sold from Africa,
but millions of African Americans were still enslaved.

45

Sometimes, they revolted violently. Some found freedom living, marrying, and engaging in normal daily life in Native American tribes. Many blacks fled to Canada on what Americans called the Underground Railroad—an escape system run by abolitionists, free blacks, and even slaves. Southern plantation owners sent slave catchers to the northern states to try to re-enslave fugitives. After the 1850 Fugitive Slave Law, free blacks in the North were kidnapped and sold in the South.

It got worse. Pro-slavery people in the North rioted against abolitionists, burning down homes, disrupting meeting halls, and destroying printing presses. People died. The United States Postal Service refused to deliver abolitionist literature and newspapers to the South. Southern preachers claimed the Bible supported slavery and that Africans liked being enslaved.

Abolitionists stormed jails to free recaptured fugitive African Americans. American church denominations split into northern and southern groups. Blacks in the North, faced with racism even from anti-slavery preachers and abolitionists, formed their own churches and denominations, calling them "come outer" churches, because they came out of other congregations.

In the end, the southern states tried to form their own country and Americans went to war with each other from 1861 to 1865. Over six hundred thousand men—about the number of people living in Louisville, Kentucky or Sheffield, England—died in a giant Civil War over the enslavement of four million blacks— almost half the population of the entire South. President Abraham Lincoln was assassinated.

Congress finally passed three constitutional amendments abolishing slavery, prohibiting racist laws, and making black men citizens. It took two and a half years for people in the Deep South to find out they were free. On June 19, 1865, enslaved people in Galveston, Texas finally heard the Emancipation Proclamation from a Union general. African Americans have celebrated Juneteenth ever since.

LATIN AMERICA

Latin America refers to many countries south of the United States, including Mexico and all of Central and South America. By the time the Reformation was spreading across Europe, Spain was enslaving the native people groups living in the Americas. In some areas, Portugal invaded as well.

Native Americans died by the thousands of European diseases like measles. Sometimes Africans, too, only lived enslaved in Latin America for three years because the conditions—and the beatings— were so brutal. But, Africa was a big place with a lot of people, so even more Africans were kidnapped and imported to serve on Latin American plantations and in gold and silver mines. In many of the colonies, nine out of every ten people were from Africa.

Latin American people intermarried ethnically, so that there were families that were black and white, native and white, and native and black. Some blacks were enslaved while others were free. During the early 1800s, the people of Latin America all revolted together against the rule of Roman Catholic Spain and Portugal, becoming new countries that were independent from European rule.

During the wars, Spain needed more money to fight against Latin American independence, but Britain wouldn't help unless Spain stopped bringing in new Africans. So, by the mid-1820s, every Spanish American country had outlawed the slave trade. Once Spain lost their wars, emancipation swept through the new Latin American countries.

Brazil, a Portuguese territory, kept its people enslaved longer than any other country in the Americas. Brazil's Underground Railroad was not at all underground—their system of escape was literally on the railroad. By the time that slavery began to crumble, groups of enslaved people would just leave plantations. Abolitionists would put the groups on trains headed toward cities—and freedom. Brazilian soldiers and police refused to re-enslave fugitives, and by May of 1888 Brazil freed all slaves.

WORDS IN BLACK AND WHITE

About 250 years after Johann Gutenberg invented the printing press, abolitionists used his invention to reason with and persuade people to join the fight against slavery. They wrote essays and printed images of slaves asking for help. They reproduced a drawing of a slave ship filled with so many people that no one could move.

Abolitionists—both black and white—founded newspapers and printed the arguments and stories of anyone against slavery who had an argument to share or a story to tell. There were almost sixty slave narratives published between 1840 and 1860. These stories let readers experience the horrors of being kidnapped and enslaved.

Writers shared how Jesus saved them from their sins. As people read, their hearts changed.

THE SECRET
CODE FOR FAMILY

Abolitionists cared a lot about loving their neighbors as themselves. That is good and right. After all, Jesus said that the most important commandment is to love God with all your heart, soul, mind, and strength. The second most important rule Jesus gave us is to love your neighbor as yourself. The Bible tells Christians how to care for our neighbors:

- Jesus tells us to love God and to love our neighbors as ourselves.

- In the Parable of the Good Samaritan, Jesus says it is more important to be concerned with being a good neighbor than with who our neighbor is. We should treat all people as our neighbors.
- We should never do wrong to our neighbors.
- In love, we should seek the good of our neighbors.
- We are commanded to proclaim the good news of Jesus to everyone!

Now, when you have friends over to visit, do your parents treat them like they treat you? Perhaps your mom asks your buddy to take out the trash, wipe down the bathroom, and grab an onion from the refrigerator for her spaghetti before doing some math problems? Probably not. Your friends may be included in some parts of your family life, but likely your mom and dad treat your friends as guests—not as family.

Family comes with responsibility, but with certain rights and privileges as well. We love and care for our family in ways we don't usually love and care for our neighbors and friends. One day you will look back and realize you loved your sisters and brothers in ways you didn't care for your friends. Maybe it's the way you share everything, or how you work on a special surprise.

In the Bible, God tells us that all Christians are adopted by God as his own children. Isn't that amazing? All Christians—called the Church by Jesus—become a family, and God has different rules for family than he does for neighbors. Some people call these family rules the "one anothers." When the Bible tells us to do something for "one another" or the "brothers," that's like a secret code just for the Church family.

We treat our Christian brothers and sisters in an extra special way. The Bible says:

- We should lay down our lives for the brothers. That means to live sacrificially—to give from

our own possessions, time, and energy—for our Christian brothers and sisters.

- We live at peace with one another.
- We love one another as Jesus loved us—by giving all to each other.
- We show each other so much honor, it is like a contest we are determined to win.
- We bear one another's burdens.
- Toward one another, we must be: humble, gentle, patient, kind, tenderhearted, forgiving, and honest.

Those are some of the ways God wants us to love each other. Does it sound too hard to follow these rules for how to treat your Christian family? The really good news is that when you follow Jesus, God the Holy Spirit gives you strength to truly love your neighbors and one another.

You are an intelligent reader. I bet you're wondering why God's rules for loving each other are smack dab in the middle of a book about how slavery ended. Then again, you are very smart. You've probably figured out that love is an action word, not just a warm fuzzy feeling. Perhaps you noticed that kidnapping and selling other people violates God's rules for how to love others. In

Revelation 18:13, God reminds us that selling slaves is selling human souls. That is never okay with God.

Around AD 62—about thirty years after Jesus was crucified and then rose from the dead—Paul wrote a letter from a prison in Rome. All thirteen letters Paul wrote, that the Holy Spirit saved for us in the Bible, were meant to be read aloud in the gathering of the Church—where all the Christians would hear them.

The short letter Paul, with Timothy's help, wrote to his Christian brother Philemon is unique. The letter, which was still written to be read aloud to Philemon's church body, was all about one enslaved man, Onesimus. Onesimus was Philemon's bondservant—or slave. Onesimus ran away to Rome, the biggest city in the Roman Empire. That's where he met Paul.

Paul writes his letter on behalf of Onesimus, who has become a Christ-follower. Now that Onesimus is a Christian brother under the "one another" rules, Paul urges Philemon to treat Onesimus as a beloved brother. Paul promises to pay any cost Philemon thinks Onesimus owes him.

We don't know for sure how Philemon received Paul's letter, but there are clues in history that Onesimus may have been freed. We do know for sure that as the Gospel spread across the world before the Reformation and Age of Exploration, slavery began to fade. After all, you can't treat a human soul like both a slave and a brother. True followers of Christ must follow his laws for loving others—and for loving one another.

JUSTICE, PLEASE

In the Bible, judges are instructed to decide what is right in God's eyes. Judges should never take a bribe—money to influence a decision—or favor someone because they are rich or poor, black or white. Enslaved people sued for their freedom, seeking justice. Remember James Somerset? The judge called slavery odious—that means repulsive.

Thousands of American slaves won their freedom in court. In the last United States Supreme Court freedom decision, a man named Dred Scott lost his case. It was clear that—in America—the court system had decided against freedom for all. Sometimes, human judges and juries make decisions that are unjust in the eyes of God. Just because something is the law, it doesn't make it right.

AFRICA, THE
NEAR AND FAR EAST

It is important to know that the cultures and religions in the East are very different than those in the West. Many people on the eastern side of the globe did not

know or love Jesus. In the West, even people who didn't love Jesus knew of him and of his rules for believers. Jesus' commands influenced public court systems and governments and impacted private beliefs. When abolitionists reminded readers to love their neighbor as themselves and treat other Christians as brothers and sisters, everyone knew those were God's rules.

During the early 1840s, British pressure on the Muslim slave trade around the oceans of Africa and the Middle East started to have an impact. In Istanbul, the slave market was outlawed and closed in 1847. Still, in 1850 there were three people enslaved in Africa and Asia for each person enslaved in the Americas.

AFRICA

How many people are in your family? Can you imagine what it would be like to have one or two of them go missing? That's what it was like for every family in Africa.

European countries did not just colonize the Americas. After the global slave trade ended in the late 1800s, Europeans colonized Africa as well in what we call the Scramble for Africa. Europeans created new territories, growing peanuts, rubber, cloves, and coconuts. Of course, they thought they should get free labor just like they did in the plantations of the West Indies. Ten times more enslaved Africans were sent east to Muslim and Asian parts of the world than to European territories from 1850 to 1900. It was a mess.

How did this happen? Slavery was banned in Europe, and then in European territories, but French and British leaders in the African colonies hid their slave trading from their governments. In their accounting, English leaders counted slaves as cattle so no one in England would know they were really selling human souls.

Through insurrections, treaties, missionary protests, and Africa's own fugitive Underground Railroad system, much of the enslavement throughout the giant continent of Africa ended. British missionaries spoke against brutality in the Congo. Zanzibar and Nigeria won their independence and gradually emancipated people.

Have you noticed that the boundaries and leaders of countries change often through history? In West Africa, the large Muslim territory called the Sokoto Caliphate was taken over by the British in 1897. The British gradually announced the end of slavery there. One British officer traveled from place to place telling slaves they were free and should go home—and they did. Within ten years, there were 200,000 people walking out of western Africa toward home.

The same thing happened in Sudan just a couple years later. The French took over the area and abolished the slave trade—but didn't free slaves.

Well, enslaved people just left. They went home and rebuilt their villages, which had been wrecked by the slave trade. So many people walked away, it looked like the whole French colonial system might collapse. The Governor tried to send in the army. Slave owners tried to re-kidnap their slaves. Other leaders ordered troops to protect the people leaving. For ten years in the early 1900s, almost a million enslaved people just went home.

MIDDLE EAST AND INDIA

In India, the Hindu caste system divided people into four categories depending on the family they were born into. Like chattel slavery in the Americas, many Indians were born into a slave-like existence. India was a British territory, but when Britain freed all slaves in 1833, India was ignored. In the late 1800s, there were

more slaves in India than in all of the Americas. The western world referred to the way India ended slavery as the "Indian Model of Abolition." Starting with the end of the slave trade in 1860, different aspects of Indian slavery were slowly made illegal.

During the time of the Reformation, Muslim raiders often took Christian slaves from Europe, the Americas, Asia, and India. They even enslaved other Muslims from northern Africa, which angered African Muslims. After each raid on a European city, there were big surges of thousands of kidnapped people for sale in the huge slave markets found in Muslim countries.

In 1890, seventeen countries gathered at the Brussels Convention in Belgium. They agreed to

pressure Muslim countries to stop selling people. The widespread Muslim tradition of selling kidnapped women as wives was not addressed by the convention. In fact, enslaved women in the East are often not counted in slavery numbers at all. After the Brussels Act, it would be decades before many Middle Eastern countries abolished slavery.

ASIA

During the Middle Ages, people from Asia were often enslaved throughout the world. Like slavery in the ancient world, enslavement in Asia was complicated and often involved agreement from the families of those enslaved. Without church families to help in times of need, and without government assistance, families often sold children when times were tough. Parents probably thought it was better for kids to be enslaved than to starve.

Countries in Asia also followed the Indian model of abolition, gradually making slave trading difficult, then banning the selling of human souls. Eventually, slavery was outlawed in each country, but it took over one hundred years for freedom to spread.

OUT OF BONDAGE

Many enslaved people took their freedom into their own hands. They fled from their bondage and hid in communities called maroons or participated in the Underground Railroad. Running away happened so often that a Southern doctor in America diagnosed the tendency to run away as a disease, which he called *draepetomania*.

The penalties for running away were severe, so some enslaved people worked for extra money and purchased themselves, becoming their own master legally. Sometimes, abolitionists would raise money to ransom fugitive slaves. While they were opposed to the idea of buying a person or compensating owners to end slavery, abolitionists recognized slavery as kidnapping, and the money paid to free a slave was a form of ransom.

THE JUSTICE
OF GOD

Good detectives of history understand what the Bible says about God's heart for people and for justice. They know not everything is as it first appears.

Slave owners claimed that the Bible supports chattel slavery. You know the Bible forbids the slave trade, because you've seen Exodus 21:16, which says: "Whoever steals a man and sells him, and anyone found in possession of him, shall be put to death." You know that we must love our neighbor as ourselves and love our Christian brothers and sisters with a sacrificial love. What, though, is the job of a follower of Jesus? What was the job of all Christians in the time of slavery?

We can learn a lot from the Old Testament prophets about how God feels about justice. From Isaiah to Malachi in the Old Testament—God warns nations to repent and tells them what will happen if they do not turn from their sins and follow God. God also tells nations why he is angry at them. God judges nations for three main sins.

First, the people follow false gods. There is only one God—and we must worship only him. The one, true God is three persons in one: God the Father, God the Son who is Jesus, and God the Holy Spirit. This is a mystery God tells us about in the Bible.

Next, God rejects false worship. We are to worship God with right hearts before him, serving Jesus. It is important that we worship God the way he desires to be worshiped, as he tells us to worship him in his Word. Religious rituals don't mean anything to God if we don't truly love Jesus and if our traditions are not directed by God's Word.

Last, God wants us to show compassion and justice to others, especially when they are in need. In Micah 6:8, God reminds us that he has already told us what is good and what he requires from us. God wants us to do justice, love kindness, and walk humbly with our God.

Now, our hearts are slippery. We should be able to tell our hearts to love God and love others, do justice, be kind, walk humbly with God, and that should be that. But sin is always knocking at the door to our hearts, so we must keep reading God's Word. The Bible is a light in the darkness for us, and it shines God's truth over all the dark corners of our heart so sin cannot hide there. In fact, knowing God's Word keeps us from making

up strange or even wicked definitions for important words like justice and kindness—like the plantation owners and government officials did during the time of slavery.

When we read the Bible and pray, we abide in Jesus. That means we are connected to him in a living way, like a branch is connected to the vine. The wonderful thing is that when you love and seek Jesus, the Holy Spirit will grow the fruit of the Spirit in your life.

Can you list the fruit of the Spirit? Love, joy, peace, patience, kindness, goodness, faithfulness, gentleness, and self-control are the fruit listed in

Galatians 5:22-23. When you begin to think and act in love or joy or goodness, your life will naturally begin to look different. You will begin to love kindness, and do justice, and walk humbly with God.

Jesus gives us great examples of what this love for justice and compassion for our Christian brothers and sisters will look like. In Matthew 25:31-46, he is talking to his disciples about the time of judgment when Jesus will righteously judge all people. Jesus will tell some people they will inherit the kingdom. He will say to those people: "For I was hungry and you gave me food, I was thirsty and you gave me drink, I was a stranger and you welcomed me, I was naked and you clothed me, I was sick and you visited me, I was in prison and you came to me" (Matthew 25:35-36).

Of course, anyone hearing this will be confused, because no one has done all of these things for Jesus. Jesus explains: "Truly, I say to you, as you did it to one of the least of these my brothers, you did it to me" (Matthew 25:40). When Jesus says the least of these, he means those fellow Christians who are in need.

During the time of abolition, many people sacrificially loved others and sought justice for the abused and oppressed. Abolitionists pursued justice for their neighbors by reasoning with people through God's Word. They brought cases of man-stealing and slave trading to court. Fugitive slaves risked their lives to tell their own stories so people would understand the horrors of slavery. Abolitionists also hid people running to freedom and sometimes traveled to plantations to free the captives.

Every abolitionist who loved God and loved their neighbor did so sacrificially—at great risk to themselves. Doing justice, loving kindness, and walking humbly with your God looks different for each person. You can trust God to help you make the right decisions to love others each day.

THE SWORD

Christian abolitionists were mostly committed to nonviolence. As the decades dragged into centuries, some abolitionists began to rethink the idea that slaves should never fight back. Slaves lived through terrible abuse. Maybe, fighting back was just self-defense.

Slave insurrections—that means a revolt against authority—happened in many places. Haitians and Jamaicans were freed through insurrection. In other areas, fighting contributed to emancipation efforts.

Slavery was abolished in the United States only through a massive civil war. The United States could have ransomed every single American slave for just one-third of the cost of the Civil War. Instead, more than six hundred thousand Americans died fighting for and against the freedom of their neighbors.

THE FREEING
OF THE WHOLE WORLD

The sad truth is that slavery has not ended. Like all sin, it still lurks in the shadows. The Bible tells us that all people sin and fall short of the glory of God—we cannot live up to God's perfect standard. We all need to follow Jesus in order to be forgiven.

The work that God's people did during abolition—when they fought to abolish slavery—spread throughout the world and many people were freed. That was a very good thing! Still, the hearts of men are wicked. This is what King Solomon meant when he said there is nothing new under the sun.

During the 1900s, the whole world went to war—twice—and slavery reared its ugly head again.

WORLD WAR I | 1914-1918

During the First World War, Germany and Russia brought slavery back to life. In Russia, over two million Germans and Austria-Hungarians were forced to work. Meanwhile, German leaders enslaved up to eight million people and made them labor for the war efforts. For instance, the abusive enslavement of hundreds of thousands of French and Belgian citizens in wartime conditions left many dead or permanently disabled.

SOVIET GULAGS

Russia became the Soviet Union in 1922 as it took over fourteen additional countries. As the First World War ended, the Soviets began establishing gulags—prison-work camps in the far-off forests of Russia. Suffering under cruel slave labor in freezing places like Siberia was supposed to re-educate prisoners in the ways of the Communist Party.

By 1928, Joseph Stalin reorganized the farming system of Russia. Farmers were sent to farm in areas much too cold to grow crops. This left areas that grew good food without enough experienced farmers. Farmers rebelled against the system, which made no sense. So, hundreds of thousands of peasants were sentenced to gulags or moved to remote locations. As a result, many people starved from a lack of food.

At the beginning of the Second World War, over two million Russians were enslaved with little objection from the rest of the world. During the war, hundreds of thousands of enslaved Soviets died of starvation. In just over thirty years, the number of slaves in Russia grew to around eighteen million human souls. After the death of Stalin in 1953, the gulags were progressively disbanded—though two gulags were still operating in the middle of the 1970s.

WORLD WAR II | 1939-1949

Fifteen years after the First World War, Germany saw the rise of Adolph Hitler's political party, the Nazis. Just as slavery during the trans-Atlantic slave trade became racial in Europe and the Americas, racism in Germany led to racial slavery in the mid-1900s. The Nazi party declared some races were only good for the most grueling jobs. Germany also decided to take over Europe. Nazi leaders wanted to control a territory as big as the North American continent. The world was at war again. It was a disaster.

The Germans enslaved a lot of people during World War II. In fact, the first five years of the war, the Germans kidnapped so many Europeans and brought them into Germany that it matched the number of Africans shipped to the New World during the trans-Atlantic slave trade. Millions and millions of Europeans were enslaved by the Nazi party, starting with the races the Germans hated most—Slavic and Polish people, and Russians. It gets worse. The Nazi party decided two races should not be enslaved, but killed. Jews and Gypsies were horribly killed in concentration camps—prison camps where people were executed. Outside Germany, tens of thousands of European children aged ten and up were enslaved making weapons of war for the Nazis.

You remember, of course, that the whole world was at war. In Asia, Japan was invading many eastern countries. The Japanese forced people into labor in Japanese coal mines, building railroads in Burma and Java,

and serving the Japanese military as they attacked more nations. Millions and millions of children, young women, and men were forced into slavery in Asia during the Second World War.

By the end of the Second World War, millions of slaves were freed—and millions of people had died. Slavery—the ugly, horrible sin that harms God's image bearers—had chained more people than during the time of abolition. This time, though, the whole world went to war against the idea that some of God's image bearers were worth more than others. Everyone fought for freedom.

By 1975, when your grandparents were alive, most countries of the world had agreed that slavery was wrong and should be ended. Sadly, there are still slaves in the world today—particularly in Africa and the Middle East.

During the time of abolition, only one out of every twenty-three people in the whole world was free. Can you imagine? That would be like having maybe only one person in your Sunday School class be free while the rest are enslaved. The good news is that today ninety-nine out of every hundred people are free. There is still work to do as we learn to love our neighbors as ourselves. but we have much to thank abolitionists for. They truly loved God and loved his people.

SETTING THE CAPTIVES FREE

Thousands of years ago, God spoke through his prophet Isaiah. He promised to send a Messiah—a Savior—who would one day bring good news to the poor, put band-aids on the brokenhearted, and announce freedom for the captives. During his ministry, Jesus read God's promise from the book of Isaiah, and announced that God's Word had been fulfilled through him.

Jesus is the Messiah whom God promised would free the captives. The truth is, we are all slaves to sin and death. But, Jesus took the punishment of all who love and follow him on the cross. Everyone who repents and follows Jesus is free from the punishment for sin. Our Messiah Jesus really has freed every captive for all eternity.

TIMELINE

1420

Prince Henry the Navigator colonizes Porto Santo in the Canary Islands and begins growing sugar cane.

1444

The first Portuguese expedition kidnap 240 people Africans for enslavement.

1453

The Turks capture Constantinople.

1455

The Gutenberg Bible is the first major book to be produced by the printing press.

1492

Christopher Columbus sails from Spain and finds the Bahamas, Cuba, and Haiti.

1494

Spain and Portugal agree on the Line of Demarcation which lets each country place themselves in charge of half of the non-Western globe. Pope Julius II approves the slave trade, saying it will help convert non-Christians to Catholicism.

1509

Roman Catholic Bishop Las Casas begins the slave trade, directing Spanish settlers to bring slaves from Africa to the New World.

1517

Martin Luther posts The Ninety-Five Theses, kicking off the Reformation.

1521

Hernando Cortes destroys the Aztec Empire and takes over Mexico.

1525-1550

Natives in Latin America are enslaved in mines.

1525-1765

Muslims import over 2 million slaves from South and Southeast Asia.

1533

Six thousand Nicaraguan Indian slaves die in one episode of measles.

1573

Diego de Arieda proposes taking Filipino slaves for New Spain.

1601

Asians from China, Japan, and the Philippines forced to work in mines.

1620-1830

One hundred thousand Hindus enslaved in Bali.

1640-1660

During the English Civil War, 12,000 Irish, English, and Scottish royalists taken into slavery in the West Indies.

By 1650

Over one million Christians are enslaved by Muslims in the Mediterranean.

1670-1690

Enslaved Native Americans replace the use of indentured European servants in British territories.

1683

In one battle, the Ottomans take 80,000 Austrians as slaves.

Late 1600s

Almost 30,000 Africans per year taken to slavery in the New World.

1700-1750

50,000 Africans enslaved each year.

1730s – 1740s

The First Great Awakening brings the gospel to people in Britain and the British American colonies.

1750-1800

75,000 Africans per year enslaved.

1761

Portugal bans the import of new enslaved people.

1763

Slaves revolt in Dutch Berbice.

1772

In British court case Somerset vs. Stewart, Justice Mansfield declares slavery is hateful, and blacks must be freed.

Arthur Young reports that out of 775 million people on earth, only 33 million are free.

1775-1783

The American Revolution takes place as American colonists fight Britain.

1777

The Police de Noirs decision makes slavery in French territories racial. The U.S., Portugal, and Spain adopt similar policies.

1778

Joseph Knight's Scottish court case bans slaves on the British mainland.

1788

Britain launches an inquiry into the slave trade.

1789-1799

The French Revolution results in the death of 20,000 French.

1790-1840

The Second Great Awakening focused on social reform for Christians.

1792

Denmark allows new enslavement for ten more years.

1794

France abolishes slavery, but reinstitutes slavery under Napoleon—twice.

1802

Norway bans the slave trade.

1804

Haiti becomes an independent country, freeing all citizens.

1807

Britain and the United States ban the slave trade.

1807-1819

Britain seizes forty-three slave ships.

1810

Venezuela prohibits the slave trade.

1813

Argentina emancipates slaves entering the country.

1819

Britain declares all enslaved people entering Canada are free.

1820

Slavery abolished in every Spanish country in Latin and Central America.

1823

Slaves in Chile freed.

1825

Uruguay emancipates all slaves.

1831-1832

Plantations burn during the Jamaican Great Baptist War.

1834

Britain frees 800,000 slaves.

1838

The British apprenticeship system is abolished.

1840

The First World Anti-slavery Convention takes place in London.

1847

Istanbul abolishes its public slave market.

1860

The Indian Penal Code makes selling or intending to sell humans illegal.

1861-1865

The American Civil War ends slavery in the United States.

1863

The Dutch emancipate West Indian slaves.

1870

Cuba gives freedom to all children in the womb. The next year, all slaves born after 1871 are free.

1873

Slavery is abolished in Puerto Rico.

1886

After slaves flee Brazilian plantations on the railroad, Cuba frees slaves.

1888

Brazil frees all slaves.

The Brussels Convention declares anti-slavery the standard of the West.

1896

France ends slavery in Madagascar.

1897

Zanzibar and northern Nigeria emancipated.

1903

West African slave markets closed.

1905-1910

Hundreds of thousands of enslaved Sudanese stream to their homes and rebuild their towns.

1914-1918

World War I results in more than 700,000 civilians being imprisoned in Germany.

1918

Russia opens the first gulag.

1920

Britain abolishes slavery in the frontier areas of Africa.

1923

Ethiopia abolishes slavery.

1939-1944

Twelve million Europeans are enslaved in Germany.

1941

Russia holds nearly two and a half million slaves in gulags. Millions of enslaved are not included in the count.

1945

The Nazi labor system collapses.

1946

African abolitionists demand France end slavery in Africa.

1948

Slavery is condemned as a violation of human rights by the United Nations.

2016

Around 40.3 million people are enslaved globally, mostly in Africa and the Middle East.

WORKS CONSULTED

Anonymous, ed. The Great Abolitionists: Sojourner Truth, John Brown, William Lloyd Garrison, Harriet Beecher Stowe, Frederick Douglass, Harriet Tubman. A.J. Cornell Publications, 2019.

Blight, David, ed. Passages to Freedom: The Underground Railroad in History and Memory. Harper Paperbacks, 2006.

Bordewich, Fergus M. Bound for Canaan: The Epic Story of the Underground Railroad, America's First Civil Rights Movement. Amistad, 2006.

Deibert, Brannon. "Who Are the Quakers? 7 Facts About Their History & Beliefs." Christianity.com. https://www.christianity.com/church/denominations/the-quakers-7-things-about-their-history-beliefs.html. Accessed 5/24/2022.

Drescher, Seymour. Abolition: A History of Slavery and Antislavery. Cambridge University Press, 2009.

Duncan, Dr. Ligon. "Defending the Faith; Denying the Image: 19th Century American Confessional Calvinism in Faithfulness and Failure" Gospel Reformation Network. May 16, 2018. https://gospelreformation.net/defending-the-faith-denying-the-image/. Accessed 9/20/2020.

Duncan, Dr. Ligon. "What About Slavery?" Reformed Theological Seminary. https://rts.edu/resources/what-about-slavery/. Accessed 9/20/2020.

Franklin, John Hope and Moss, Alfred A., Jr. From Slavery to Freedom: A History of African Americans. McGraw-Hill Higher Education, 2000.

Grun, Bernard. The Timetables of History. Simon & Schuster, 1963.

"Global Findings." Global Slavery Index. https://www.globalslaveryindex.org/2018/findings/global-findings/. Accessed 5/17/2022.

Grudem, Wayne. Systematic Theology: An Introduction to Biblical Doctrine. Zondervan, 1995, pp. 442-443.

Hudson, J. Blaine. Encyclopedia of the Underground Railroad. McFarland & Company, 2006.

Menikoff, Aaron. "How and Why Did Some Christians Defend Slavery?" The Gospel Coalition. February 24, 2017. https://www.thegospelcoalition.org/article/how-and-why-did-some-christians-defend-slavery/. Accessed 9/20/2020.

Newman, Richard S. Abolitionism: A Very Short Introduction. Oxford University Press, 2018.

Ross, Mark. "Imago Dei." Ligonier. March 25, 2013. https://www.ligonier.org/learn/articles/imago-dei. Accessed 6/5/2022.

Sharp, Joshua. "Voices: There is no biblical defense for American slavery" Baptist Standard. January 27, 2020. https://www.baptiststandard.com/opinion/voices/no-biblical-defense-american-slavery/. Accessed 9/20/2020.

Sinha, Manisha. The Slave's Cause: A History of Abolition. Yale University Press, 2016.

Still, William, and Quincy T. Mills, editor. The Underground Railroad Records: Narrating the Hardships, Hairbreadth Escapes, and Death Struggles of Slaves in Their Efforts for Freedom. Modern Library, 2019.

Walters, Kerry, Ed. Let Justice Be Done: Writings from American Abolitionists 1688-1865. Orbis Books, 2020.

Special thanks to Pastor Chris LeDuc of Cannon Beach Bible Church and his Bible study class for all your thoughts on the Bible and its application to our lives.

Danika has done it again! Built on the foundation of God's command to love our neighbors as ourselves, in her Who, What, Why series, Danika comprehensively explores the tragic history of slavery throughout time and throughout the world. It's a sad history, but also a hopeful one, with God's gracious promise ultimately to set captives free.

Douglas Bond
Author of more than thirty books,
including *War in the Wasteland,* and *The Resistance*

Danika Cooley illustrates for us that the biblical truth that all human beings are made in the image of God is revolutionary. God used this truth to sting the consciences of many people into action during the days of slavery and the slave trade. Their indifference was turned into outrage, and they become abolitionists. It was a long fight, but victory was finally won. May young people reading this book go on to be reformers in areas that need the light of God today!

Conrad Mbewe
Pastor of Kabwata Baptist Church and founding chancellor of the African Christian University in Lusaka, Zambia

Danika Cooley had hit the mark with this series. Slavery is an ugly topic, but the stories of the Christian responses to the evil allow hope to shine through. Readers will learn a lot of history, but more importantly they will learn what it means to put the Gospel into action. A series well worth reading.

Linda Finlayson
Author of *God's Timeline* and *God's Bible Timeline*

Other books in the series

Why did the Reformation Happen?
Danika Cooley

The Church was following the words of men rather than the Word of God but brave men read God's Word and were saved from their sins. They fought for truth against the most powerful organizations of the time – the Church and the Crown. Danika Cooley explores how God's people changed the Church, Europe and the World. This is the story of how the Church found the gospel and the people heard about Christ.

ISBN: 978-1-5271-0652-9

Who was Martin Luther?
Danika Cooley

Martin Luther was a young man who was afraid of a thunderstorm. He was a monk seeking for salvation. He was a reformer who inspired a continent to return to the Word of God. Danika Cooley introduces 9–11 year olds to this key figure in the Reformation.

ISBN: 978-1-5271-0650-5

What was the Gutenberg Bible?
Danika Cooley

Johann Gutenberg invented a world–changing machine that meant people could read God's Word for themselves. The world could share ideas, discoveries and new and God's Word could be quickly, inexpensively and accurately reproduced. Danika Cooley helps 9–11 year–olds discover how the printing press paved the way for the Reformation.

ISBN: 978-1-5271-0651-2

CHRISTIAN FOCUS PUBLICATIONS

Christian Focus | Christian Heritage | CF4K | Mentor

CF4·K
Because you're never
too young to know Jesus

Christian Focus Publications publishes books for adults and children under its four main imprints: Christian Focus, CF4K, Mentor and Christian Heritage. Our books reflect our conviction that God's Word is reliable and Jesus is the way to know him, and live for ever with him.

Our children's publication list covers pre-school to early teens. We also publish personal and family devotional titles, biographies and inspirational stories that children will love.

From pre-school board books to teenage apologetics, we have it covered!

Christian Focus Publications Ltd,
Geanies House, Fearn, Ross-shire,
IV20 1TW, Scotland,
United Kingdom.
www.christianfocus.com